At Break of Day

A play

Noël Greig

Samuel French — London
New York - Toronto - Hollywood

AT BREAK OF DAY

First produced by theatre nomad and opened at The Fringe Studio as part of the Hong Kong City Festival on 26th January, 2000. The production subsequently toured England. The cast was as follows:

Soldier One   Paul Huntley-Thomas
Soldier Two/Father/Guide   Jean Pagni
Girl/Mother/Militia/Cop Two   Hannah Buvik
Woman/Daughter/Archaeologist Two/Cop One
                                         Paola Cavallin
Man/Brother/Archaeologist One/Prisoner
                          Louise Barrett/Ayo Oyelami

Directed by Luke Dixon
Designed by Luke Dixon and Joanie Magill
Movement by Jane Turner
Assistant Director Ramiro Silveira

CHARACTERS

Soldier One
Soldier Two
Goatboy
Mother ⎫
Daughter ⎬ the Goatboy's family
Father ⎭
Girl
Woman
Man
Tour Guide
Archaeologist One
Archaeologist Two
A person from the Militia
Guard: in the prison
Prisoner
Cop One ⎫
⎬ military policemen
Cop Two ⎭

It is suggested that the actors playing **Soldier One, Soldier Two, Girl** and **Woman** should not double other parts.

The action of the play takes place in various interior and exterior settings.

The interval is optional. If no interval is taken, the playing time is approximately one hour and forty minutes.

AUTHOR'S NOTE

The play is suitable for work with young people aged fifteen and above. Since its first production I have used it in schools and with youth groups. It can be approached without detailed research into specific historical events it refers to, as a tale in the *Alice* tradition. For teachers and youth-leaders who also wish to use it as a resource, then the process can include looking at those events which echo through the story: the two World Wars, post-communist Eastern Europe, Palestine, archaeological finds, Tianamen Square, the Holocaust, et cetera.

The original production was played out on an open stage with very little in the way of setting: a couple of stepladders, a large piece of cloth, a string of bells, a constant lighting state. The costumes were loose tunics and bare feet, with minimal add-ons to indicate fresh characters. In this publication of the script there are indications of setting and lighting changes, which will hopefully be used if a more complex production is being planned. My advice, though, is to create a physical world for the play that does not detract from nor interrupt the fluid, dreamlike quality of the story.

Noël Greig

Other plays by Noël Greig published by Samuel French Ltd

Do We Ever See Grace?
Rainbow's Ending

N.B.

There is no sheet music available for the song on page 1.

ACT I
SCENE 1

A scarred landscape. A long dusty road on the way from the south to the north

When the play begins, the light is bright, with no shade

Soldier One, in a filthy uniform, is cooking up some food in a battered tin can over a fire, stirring it with a spoon. His canvas knapsack and heavy rifle are by his side

Soldier One (*singing to himself*)
>The sun comes up
>The sun goes down
>And the wicked old world
>Goes round and round
>The wicked old world goes round.
>Some time you're born
>Some time you'll die
>And in between you laugh and cry.
>The thinkers think
>But their feet still stink
>The rich wear gold
>But they still grow old
>And we all rot together under the sky
>We all rot together under the ground.
>The sun comes up
>The sun goes down
>And the wicked old ...

Soldier Two enters carrying a knapsack and rifle. His worn, filthy uniform is in a different style from One's, perhaps that of a foreign battalion

The two men stare at each other for several moments. Soldier One carefully takes out a packet of cigarettes

Soldier One Smoke?
Soldier Two It would be a pleasure.
Soldier One "A pleasure!"

Soldier Two I say it wrong?
Soldier One I like it. "It would be a pleasure."
Soldier Two That is correct?
Soldier One Very correct. Very proper.
Soldier Two Thank you.
Soldier One But I'd not say that. If someone offered me a ciggie. I'd say — "sure."
Soldier Two "Shaw".
Soldier One So. (*Proffering the cigarettes*) Ciggie?
Soldier Two Shaw! (*He takes one*)

Soldier One lights a match. Soldier Two tries to light his cigarette but his hand shakes

Soldier One Keep your hand steady. That's a bad shake. Here, give it back, I'll light it for you. (*He takes the cigarette from Soldier Two*) There. (*He lights the cigarette and hands it back*) That'll calm you down.

Soldier Two attempts to raise the cigarette to his mouth

No, no. It'll end up in your ear. Give it here.

Soldier Two hands over the cigarette. Soldier One holds the cigarette while Soldier Two smokes

Now open your mouth. Good long draw. Good. Again. Better?
Soldier Two Better.
Soldier One We'll share it.

They smoke in silence, with Soldier One keeping hold of the cigarette

Was it the fighting? Brought on the shakes?
Soldier Two I have not eaten for some length of time.
Soldier One "Length of time". You speak like a schoolbook.
Soldier Two In my country we learned your language in the school.
Soldier One Good fighters, your lot.

They smoke in silence

Soldier Two We made the battles on the same side?
Soldier One Some of the years, maybe.
Soldier Two That first year, I think …
Soldier One Yes?

Soldier Two I am forgetting.
Soldier One Me too. No matter. All over now. Grub then?
Soldier Two "Grub"?
Soldier One My little pot. Spoon. Dig in.

Soldier One picks up the tin can, peers into it, then puts it back

Soldier Two My sincere apologies.
Soldier One Good grub.
Soldier Two Grubs would not sit in my stomach.
Soldier One Not grubs. Grub.
Soldier Two One grub only? Perhaps if I take it out …
Soldier One Took what out?
Soldier Two The grub. If I take it out, then I may eat the food. (*He fishes in the pot with the spoon*) You will eat the grub? Is it very big?
Soldier One My friend, you're not well. I should've known from the shakes. You're light-headed. The sooner you get some food down you the better. (*He takes the spoon*) We'll do it like the cigarette. You open and I'll spoon it in.
Soldier Two But no grub!
Soldier One This *is* the grub!
Soldier Two No, no … What word? … Ah, yes — *maggot!* Yes! Take *maggot* out first. Maggot will not stay in me.
Soldier One Oh! Right! Got you …
Soldier Two You understand?
Soldier One *That* sort of grub.
Soldier Two So you eat grub, then I eat food.
Soldier One It's not creepy-crawly grub. Food *is* grub. Grub another word for food. Forget maggot.
Soldier Two Food — grub — same. No maggot.
Soldier One Correct.
Soldier Two That was not in the schoolbook.
Soldier One Now eat.
Soldier Two (*eating*) Three days, no food. I was separated from my battalion. You know the last big fighting? Around the cathedral?
Soldier One Little mouthfuls.
Soldier Two All of the enemy were dead. It was over. I could not find my friends.
Soldier One Hey! *I'm* not dead!
Soldier Two The grub is good.
Soldier One If I'm not dead, we must have been on the same side.
Soldier Two I ate some roots, but they would not stay in me.
Soldier One (*producing a tin water bottle*) And now some little swigs of this.

They eat and drink in silence for a few moments

(*Taking out a ragged cloth map*) And now. The way home.

Soldier One pores over the map, looking up and out occasionally. Soldier Two produces a small notebook and pencil

(*Turning the map different ways*) Which way, which damned way?
Soldier Two (*looking at the map and then at the landscape*) The long valley there. It could be this place on the map. And we sit on this road — here.
Soldier One Good chap.
Soldier Two Maybe. Or the river — (*he points the other way*) may be — (*he points at the map*) this river here.
Soldier One Maybe?
Soldier Two Maybe. Which direction for you?
Soldier One North.
Soldier Two North for me.
Soldier One But look at it. Bloody wilderness. We could start out up that valley and end up where we began. Or follow that river and finish up back at that cathedral. And it's getting dark.
Soldier Two When the morning comes. We will decide. Now we sleep.
Soldier One North or south? We still won't know.
Soldier Two Wait. (*He produces a compass*) Compass …
Soldier One Good man. A bullet got mine. Used to keep it here. (*He pats his chest pocket*) Saved my life, that did. So, you've the compass, I've the map. We're a team. Problem solved. Kip down now.
Soldier Two "Kip?"
Soldier One Sleep.
Soldier Two Ah. (*He writes in his notebook*) "Kip." What other words for sleep?
Soldier One Let's see … Snooze …
Soldier Two (*writing*) Snooze.
Soldier One Doze.
Soldier Two Doze.
Soldier One (*yawning*) Shut-eye.
Soldier Two Shut-eye.
Soldier One Bye-byes.
Soldier Two Bye-byes.
Soldier One (*yawning*) Forty winks.
Soldier Two Forty winks. Forty winks?
Soldier One To — (*he yawns*) — dream.
Soldier Two Ah. I know "dream".

Soldier One In — the — Land — of — Nod. (*He falls asleep*)
Soldier Two "What dreams may come,
           When we have shuffled off this mortal coil,
           Aye, there's the rub."
           (*He yawns and sleeps*)

The Lights fade

SCENE 2

A dusty park in a drab city

A young Girl with a backpack sits on the ground. She takes out a street map and peers at it

A Woman enters and squats beside the Girl

Woman You are looking for?
Girl Oh. Somewhere I heard of.
Woman You show. (*She takes the map*) This map too old. Look. Here this park. But different name. Streets also. All different names. Where you look for?
Girl Why are they different? The names?
Woman After the Great Change.
Girl The — "Great Change"?
Woman The song of the future. Ha! You have cigarette for me?
Girl You shouldn't do that.
Woman See statue? In centre of the park? Leader. This park is now named for him. Why you come here?
Girl What was it called? Before the Great Change?
Woman Strangers do not come here. Too dry, too dusty. Nothing. That cracked marble over there. It was a fountain with water once. Once there were beds of flowers. You want tourist route, you want coastline. Hotel, beach, disco. No such things here. Nothing for your money here.
Girl The name of this park before? What was it?
Woman Name of a king. Some king.
Girl Yes. A king. Here. (*She produces a worn notebook — Soldier Two's notebook, but many years old*) That king?
Woman You write this?
Girl My great-grandfather.
Woman Some of the words. My language.
Girl I don't know those words. What's that one? He uses that one a lot.
Woman It is my word for "dream".

Girl Look. He says his home was a house near the park named after the king. Could this be the park?

Woman Rich people had homes here. In those big places. Before the Great Change.

Girl (*reading*) "Today I—*dream*—of walking home through the park after school, smelling the blossom, listening to the water splashing in the fountains. The sunlight falling through the green leaves. I wonder if I will ever see that again."

Woman They ran away. The rich people. Did he run away, your great-grandfather?

Girl He still fought for his country when the war came. He may have emigrated, but he was still loyal to his country in his heart.

Woman Perhaps they took the flowers and the water with them.

Girl I just wanted to see it.

Woman The place he ran away from?

Girl Stop saying "ran away".

Woman Dust now.

Girl My family told me he disappeared, after the war.

Woman Dried up.

Girl What a stupid thing to do.

Woman Running away?

Girl Stupid of me to come here. I thought it would make me feel different.

Woman Different?

Girl Give me a sense of … I hate where I live.

Woman You hate your home?

Girl It's so — artificial.

Woman Arti —— ?

Girl Made up. Pretend. No roots. Big lawns, always green, but the water is piped in from the mountains. Everyone drives. No little shops and people talking on the street corner. Huge covered places on the edge of the town, with music and things to buy from all over the world. I hoped that if I came here I would … Oh well, never mind.

A Man strolls in. He stands some way off, smoking a cigarette

Woman Give me your hand. I will tell your fortune.

Girl You can do that? (*She holds out her right hand*)

Woman No. Left.

Girl (*holding out her left hand*) Why the left?

Woman (*taking the Girl's hand*) The left tells you what is to come.

Girl And the right?

Woman Tells you what you are doing.

The Man whistles a tune

Girl (*looking around*) What a waste of money.
Woman (*looking at the Girl's hand*) Yes … Yes …
Girl You're holding me too tight.
Woman To keep you steady.
Girl Even so …
Woman Be still.
Girl But it hurts …
Woman Will not be long.
Girl Hurts.

The Man suddenly runs across and puts his hand over the Girl's mouth

Woman (*holding the left hand*) You will be repaying a debt.

The Woman and the Man carry the Girl off

The Lights fade

SCENE 3

The dusty road. Dawn

The scene looks cold. Soldier One and Soldier Two are asleep on the ground, curled up together like spoons. Soldier Two's notebook lies by him

Soldier One wakes and disentangles himself. He stands up, shivers and rubs himself to get warm. He looks out across the landscape

Soldier One Which way? Which way? (*He picks up Soldier Two's notebook and flicks through it; reading*) "If I fight for my country, perhaps my country will fight for me." (*He flicks further; reading*) "I have learned the word for 'hope' in this language. I hope that I will not forget how to say it in my own language." (*He flicks further; reading*) "Kip. Snooze. Doze. Shut-eye. Bye-byes. Forty winks."

Soldier Two sits up suddenly, shivering

Soldier Two Dream!
Soldier One Welcome to the world.
Soldier Two It was terrible.
Soldier One Tell me.
Soldier Two It is leaving me.
Soldier One Speak it fast.
Soldier Two Home.

Soldier One Describe.
Soldier Two Going back … Someone went back …
Soldier One Good, good …
Soldier One Terrible …
Soldier Two "Home sweet home." Don't tell me what home is.
Soldier One "There's no place like home."
Soldier Two You know nothing!
Soldier One "Home is where the heart is."
Soldier Two Now I have forgotten the dream, with all your stupid talk of home. I don't have to walk along the road with all of that in my ears. Ignorant pig! (*He marches away from Soldier One*)
Soldier One Suit yourself. I don't want to spend the journey explaining every damn word. Foreign git! (*He marches off in the other direction*)

They both stop, look around them, then turn and look at each other

Soldier Two (*producing the compass*) So … ?
Soldier One (*producing the map*) So … ?

A pause

    Look, I …
Soldier Two No, please …
Soldier One Hope you don't think I was …
Soldier Two You weren't to know, and I was …
Soldier One All right, all right …
Soldier Two Yes, yes, all right.
Soldier One And this. (*He holds up the notebook*) No good to me. Being nosey. You don't mind?
Soldier Two (*taking the notebook*) No-sey?
Soldier One Nose-ey. (*He mimes being nosey*)
Soldier Two Inquisitive?
Soldier One *Educated* foreign git.
Soldier Two "Git"?
Soldier One Here we go … Well … Twerp — bonehead — idiot.
Soldier Two (*writing*) Git. I like.
Soldier One "Git" is an insult.
Soldier Two I called you pig.
Soldier One Then we're squits.
Soldier Two "Squits"?
Soldier One No! If we carry on like this we'll be here till the crack of doom. Let's go. Which way? River, valley or road?
Soldier Two All the same risk.

Soldier One My map, your compass. Our choice. How?

Soldier Two (*picking up three pebbles*) This red stone: river. This white
 stone: valley. This black stone: road. Now we both close eyes.

They both close their eyes

 (*Throwing one stone away*) One gone. (*He puts his hands behind his back*)
 Open eyes.

They do

 Now, one stone in left, one in right. You choose.

Soldier One Left.

Soldier Two (*opening his hand*) Valley.

Soldier One Down the valley it is, then.

They look out

Soldier Two Last evening, it was — different.

Soldier One Yes … But maybe it was the light.

Soldier Two Maybe. But — not the same. Not so much brown earth.

Soldier One The sun was going down. Things look different in that light.

Soldier Two There was some green in the distance. Where has the green
 gone to?

Soldier One Same valley, though. Push on, eh?

They make to go

There is the sound of distant goatbells

Goatboy (*off*) Hey! Hey!

Soldier One and Soldier Two stop

 The Goatboy runs on

Goatboy Did you see them?

Soldier One Who?

Goatboy My goats. I lost six last week. If this goes on my family will be
 starving within the month.

Soldier One (*pointing*) Your goats are over there.

Goatboy They are not the lost goats. Where are the three I lost? Did you see
 them? If they get under that wire I've lost them.

Soldier One What wire?

Goatboy (*pointing*) That barbed wire *there*. Haven't you got eyes in your head!

Soldier One (*to Soldier Two*) Can you see any barbed wire?

Soldier Two Well, no ... But ... Yes, yes — maybe there is barbed wire. Was it there last night?

Soldier One No ... Well ... Maybe. (*To the Goatboy*) We definitely saw no goats. What happens if they've gone under the wire?

Goatboy The bastards get them.

Soldier One The bastards?

Goatboy You're not with the bastards?

Soldier One We're with each other.

Soldier Two Should we look for the goats? Under the wire?

Goatboy I only go under the wire at night.

Soldier Two Why?

Goatboy Where've you been? Because the bastards will *shoot*, of course.

Soldier Two You have never seen me at work. Down on my belly, in amongst the rocks, through the grass, I'm a lizard. You see ... I will crawl under that wire. (*He crawls in the direction the Goatboy pointed*)

Soldier One Bloody fool. The war is over.

Soldier Two He said his family will starve. They need the goats.

Soldier One What's that to us?

Soldier Two We may need friends.

Soldier Two crawls off

Soldier One Suit yourself. Get dead. I'm not sticking around for more shoot-ups.

Goatboy Your friend, he is going under the wire.

Soldier One Bloody liability. (*Shouting*) Li-a-bil-ty! Know what that means? I'm off!

Goatboy He's a real lizard.

Soldier One Damn!

Goatboy Look. You cannot tell where he is.

Soldier One He's got the bloody compass!

Goatboy He's invisible ...

Soldier One (*calling*) Hey! Chuck the compass over the wire.

No reply

The compass! Chuck it over the wire! If they bag you, I'm stuck.

No reply. A shot

Shit! So. Nothing else for it. (*He crawls on his belly in the same direction as that taken by Soldier Two*)
Goatboy Even if you only get one of the goats.
Soldier One It's the compass I'm after, not the damn goats.

Soldier One crawls off

The Goatboy watches Soldier One go

There is a shot

After a moment the Goatboy collects up the rifles and the knapsacks and leaves in the other direction

The Lights fade

SCENE 4

A room

The Girl is blindfolded

Girl Just because we have green lawns doesn't mean … It might seem rich to you, but … My government has a strict policy on hostages. There was too much of it. They refuse to give in. Unless it's diplomatic. This is not diplomatic. This is … Please. I do understand, I do. I can take money out on my cards. Can you hear me? What have I done to you? I've not harmed you. I'm not an animal.

The Lights fade

SCENE 5

The dusty road

Soldier One and Soldier Two are lying on the ground. Soldier One sits up. He rubs his head. Soldier Two sits up. He feels his chest

Soldier One That was a close shave.
Soldier Two I was having that dream.
Soldier One Spare me your dreams.
Soldier Two Someone could not see. I tried to find them, to hold up a lamp for them in the dark.

Soldier One "The light of the world." Now what was that?
Soldier Two Is it the dawn or the dusk?

They look out

Soldier One Some in-between time. Purple time. (*He thinks for a moment*) Got it. It was the Son of God. There was a picture of him. "The light of the world". Purple cloak and a lamp. It used to hang in our back kitchen.
Soldier Two Where?
Soldier One My … No, I'm not using the word, it sends you funny.
Soldier Two It won't kill me.
Soldier One Home. Home.
Soldier Two Makes you sad?
Soldier One Want to be there.
Soldier Two You will. I will see us there. Home.
Soldier One See, you're still breathing.
Soldier Two (*feeling his chest*) For a little moment I wasn't sure.
Soldier One "Little moment". I like that. How little is it?
Soldier Two It is—(*he places his hand on Soldier One's heart then removes it*) that.
Soldier One And a big moment?
Soldier Two In that last fighting, around the cathedral. When we got to the end of the war. I took aim and a face exploded in front of me. One moment it was staring at me and its mouth was working. Then it stopped. It could have been a smile or a scream. Either. It stopped working. It hung there. As does the cow's head on the butcher's rack. Staring at me. Then it slowly came apart, from the middle. As they say the universe began, moving out from the middle. In the silence of space. Beautiful. All the colours. White bone, green matter, blood, grey substance. Floating away from the centre. A few seconds perhaps, but a long moment.

There is the sound of goatbells. They look towards the sound

Soldier One There they are. A mother and two little ones. Trotting towards us. (*Calling gently*) Here, little goats. You want to go home? Had enough of the wandering life? Here they come.
Soldier Two (*holding his head*) She was looking for someone's home. Then she was in a dark place.
Soldier One (*to the goats*) Come … come … (*He crawls away towards them*)
Soldier Two (*curling up*) Wake me when you have them.
Soldier One Little goats …

Soldier One exits

Soldier Two Going home … (*He falls asleep*)

The Lights fade

SCENE 6

A house with an earth floor

The Father is sleeping on the floor. The Mother and the Goatboy squat on the floor, inspecting the two knapsacks. The Daughter is sitting on a chair. In contrast to the others she is dressed in city clothes. She is eating with her fingers

Goatboy It is no lie, Mother. I heard the shots. They've no use for them now.
Mother You'll get us all hanged one day. If the bastards find us with them …
Goatboy They were not with the bastards.
Mother Who then?
Goatboy They tried to rescue the goats.
Mother And where are the goats? Three more gone. Do you want to ruin us entirely? You see, daughter? What's happened while you've been away? How your brother has turned out?
Goatboy (*to the Daughter*) What's it like to eat with your fingers again, sister?
Mother Three years have not changed her. But you? How many goats have gone missing this week? We should have killed a goat, to celebrate her coming home. Good and juicy on the spit. But you lose them.
Father (*waking*) Why all this noise? (*He sees the Daughter*) Ah, there she is. My little one. Now we're a family again. Look, there's a full moon rising. My heart feels that big. Tell us about your life over there, daughter. In that city.
Goatboy Knives and forks.
Daughter You could have knives and forks, Mother.
Mother Such a dream!
Goatboy Knives and forks! The bastards could still come and kick us out tomorrow. Tear down the walls. So much for knives and forks then.
Mother (*to the Father*) Bring him to order, can't you? You sleep and dream while your son insults his mother. And see now. (*She points at the knapsacks*) Stealing from the bastards. We'll all hang.
Daughter Look here. (*She produces a folded piece of cloth. She unfolds it, revealing some banknotes*) I saved it. It was worth being away from home three years, knowing I would bring this back with me. You could buy some land. You could build a proper home.

Mother (*counting the notes*) Whoever saw so much money?

Daughter Enough for some land and proper building materials.

Goatboy You still don't get it. If the bastards decide they want to settle here, they'll move in. Kick us out. Last year they demolished a whole village. Packed everyone into carts and sent them off to another place.

Father That was just a rumour.

Mother Our own house. No more mud walls. Proper stone.

Goatboy Mother, you deserve that. But the hard truth is ——

Father Do you wish your mother to end her days not having felt her own walls around her? Not have water without a daily trek to the well?

Mother Imagine. Water coming straight into my own kitchen.

Goatboy And they own the water. It's down there, beneath us, but they own it. They can cut it off at any moment.

Daughter Father. When you wrote to me, why didn't you tell me any of this?

Goatboy They own the postal service. Do you imagine they'd let that sort of information through? What did he write about? How the peach trees were doing? How the goats were keeping? We're like goats. In a pen. When they want to shift the goats to another pen, they shift them.

Daughter But the newspapers said ——

Goatboy The newspapers!

Mother (*counting the money*) We could have a decent tiled floor.

Daughter The newspapers said there was an agreement.

Goatboy You've been away too long.

Daughter A settlement.

Goatboy You were too busy eating in the cafés, with knives and forks.

Father Saving money. For her family. Not losing goats.

Goatboy Sitting in the cafés gossiping, while we ——

Daughter I worked hard for that money. D'you think they made life easy for me? I wasn't welcomed. Not into their homes.

Mother Don't quarrel. You mustn't quarrel. Things *are* getting better, daughter. We have our own administration.

Goatboy Oh, yes. Our own administration. So when they move us on …

Father *We* have not been moved on. Whatever happened in that village was ——

Goatboy So you did hear.

Father Rumours anyway.

Goatboy (*to the Daughter*) And we've not been moved because Father is an official. If you're on the administration, you don't get moved. At least, not until …

Mother So you see, it's all right. We can build a proper home.

Goatboy A proper goat pen.

Father Don't mock your mother.

Goatboy The sun mocks my mother every day. The sun is free to move across the sky. The birds too, they mock her. They can fly wherever they want to. We need a special pass to visit the next village. Did you think the checkpoint today was a one-off, sister? An emergency? Oh yes, it's a pass which has the stamp of *our* administration on it, and it's *our* guards at the checkpoints. But look up at the top of the hills. It's *their* patrols looking down at us through the telescopes. Making sure we do it correctly. And if we try and slip through, just once, to prove that we can fly like the birds ... Look ... (*He rolls up his sleeve*). And look. (*He rolls up his trouser leg*) *Our* police have to buy their batons from them, too.

Father Your mother must decide.

Mother Decide?

Father It is your right to have your own home. But — well — there are — certain dangers. Even though I am on the administration, even though there have been advances, one can never forecast the future ...

Mother How do I decide?

Father Judge what is best. The money has to be turned into something.

Mother My own roof. Cool marble floors. A little inner courtyard with shade and a fountain.

Goatboy Or guns.

Father Silence.

Goatboy I mean, to keep the robbers out. What else would I mean? If we live in such a fine place there'll be robbers for sure.

Father There are no robbers in this village. We leave our doors unlocked at night.

The Mother divides the money into four portions and hands them out during the following

Mother My portion is for the marble tiles. You do as you wish with yours. The walls, the roof and the floor. But you can turn it into other things if you so wish. I'm not deciding for anyone else.

Daughter Can't we all come to an agreement. A general agreement. Something that will benefit us all.

There is the sound of goatbells and a knock at the door

They hide the money. The Mother opens the door

Soldier One is outside. He enters the room

There is a silence. Soldier One sees the knapsacks. He goes over to them

Soldier One The other soldier. Where is he?

Goatboy I thought you were both dead.
Soldier One I found your goats.
Mother He has done nothing. He's a good lad.
Soldier One I tied them to the peach tree.
Mother Don't take him away.
Father Sir. My son is not a thief. He may be wild and I know he gives you trouble. But not a thief. Please do not arrest him.
Soldier One Arrest him?
Father I am on the administration, sir, I ——
Soldier One Why should I arrest him? Unless of course ...
Father Look, sir. (*He produces a document*) Here is the evidence ...
Soldier One (*to the Goatboy*) What did you do to him?
Father See. The official stamp.
Soldier One You little shit. I rescue your goats and ——
Mother Sir ... sir ...
Father I am reliable, sir. My family makes no trouble. I kneel before you.
Daughter Father!
Goatboy We cringe like dogs.
Soldier One (*to the Goatboy*) Where is he?
Mother We've seen no-one else, sir.
Soldier One (*producing his map and spreading it out*) He's got the bloody compass. What'll I do? This damn map gets bigger every time. You sure you've not seen him?
Mother Let the god strike me down.
Father (*to the Mother*) Offer him something. Go on, go on ...
Mother Sir, may I give you some food?
Father Butter him up.
Mother And a bed for the night? It's getting dark. You won't want to be trudging off in the dark.
Father You can have our bed, sir.
Daughter Father!
Father Ssh. This is diplomatic.
Soldier One A bed.
Mother When did you last sleep in a bed?
Soldier One My body has forgotten.
Mother I'll make up a good soft bed for you, sir.
Father And you'd like some peaches, sir? I will pick you some myself. The best, straight from the tree.
Soldier One (*looking at the map*) It's all a puzzle.
Father Anything, anything ...

The Father leaves

Goatboy (*to the Daughter*) See what it's like.

Mother (*to the Daughter*) Wash your bowl. Then fill it up for him.
Goatboy And apologize for the lack of knives and forks.

The Mother and the Daughter exit

Soldier One So you reckoned we were goners?
Goatboy You hear a gunshot round here, someone's had it.
Soldier One On the subject of guns ——
Goatboy They don't like guns in the house. If the bastards caught us with guns in the house …
Soldier One No guns allowed?
Goatboy Not for us. That's why we need guns. Look at my father. He thought you were coming for me. What if you had been? What could we have done? Here — (*he takes out his money*) I'll buy your guns.
Soldier One It's a long road ahead. Can't risk it without a gun.
Goatboy You'll need money.
Soldier One True …
Goatboy And if the other one's cleared off …
Soldier One I was getting to like him.
Goatboy I buried them in the melon patch. In the morning I'll dig yours up. Keep his.
Soldier One Well …
Goatboy Double the offer.
Soldier One Done.

The Mother enters

Mother The bed is ready.
Soldier One (*yawning*) I could sleep for ever.
Mother If the god is willing.
Soldier One Ever and ever.

Soldier One exits

Mother I shan't rest till he's out of here.
Goatboy Oh, he's an angel.
Mother A devil.
Goatboy Bearing gifts.

The Daughter enters. She hands the Goatboy her money

Here. You decide what to spend it on.
Mother No, no — tomorrow we will …

Daughter Tomorrow I'll be gone. Tomorrow will be the same here. Tomorrow can sort for itself.
Mother (*to the Goatboy*) Fetch your father, he'll stop this nonsense.

The Goatboy exits

Daughter What can he stop? He knelt in the dust.
Mother You came at a bad moment.
Daughter This whole place is a bad moment.
Mother Your home, it's your ——
Daughter A bad dream.
Mother You wish to kill me?
Daughter I wish to save myself. Over there, in that city, there are places I have to avoid. People who call names, spit in my face. But I can still hold my head up. I think perhaps my brother is right. Guns.

The Goatboy enters. He has an untidy handful of banknotes

Mother Is he coming?
Goatboy He's out there.
Mother Picking peaches?
Goatboy Hanging from a branch. Like the peaches. Dangling. This was blowing about in the dirt. (*He holds up the money*)

The Mother exits

Daughter (*to the Goatboy*) You can decide for all of us.

The Daughter exits

The Goatboy is left alone with the money

The Lights fade

SCENE 7

The dusty road

Soldier Two lies on the ground, asleep. He wakes up suddenly

Soldier Two Did you find the goats? Did they come to your arms? I was dreaming of the goats on the moon. But there are no goats on the moon. They were being herded towards the dark side. The side where the sun never goes. Herded over the rim of the moon, across the craters of the moon. The side of the moon that is ice. Ice. Why is it so cold? Where are you? (*He shivers, curls up and sleeps*)

The Lights fade

SCENE 8

A cellar

The Girl and the Woman are on stage. The Girl is reading to the Woman from the notebook

Girl (*reading*) "I have been studying how I may compare
           This prison where I live unto the world;
           And, for because the world is populous
           And here is not a creature but myself,
           I cannot do it."

The Woman takes the book

Woman (*reading*) "I have been — studying." When is "have been"?
Girl Something you do for a time. Then you stop. Then it's in the past. The king in the play has been studying.
Woman Kings!
Girl Or something you were.
Woman "I have been a king."
Girl "I have been a prisoner."
Woman You are a prisoner. Your great-grandfather. He would have liked kings. The king tried to run away, too. He was not so lucky.
Girl Was life better after that?
Woman For a while, I am told. They changed the names of the streets. They pulled down the old statues, put up new ones. Sometimes one of the new ones would disappear. A name could not be spoken. People disappeared.
Girl Is that what your "Great Change" brought?
Woman I can speak your language. I know your word for "sneer". There was broken glass in the window-frames of the schoolhouse, but we were taught several languages. You did not even know my word for "dream".
Girl What about your word for "freedom"?
Woman If your parents love you enough.
Girl My parents love me.
Woman When they prove it, I will teach you "freedom".
Girl Do you have children? Feelings for them?
Woman "Come you spirits,
           That tend on mortal thoughts! unsex me here,
           And fill me from the crown to the toe, top full
           Of direst cruelty."
That was a queen speaking. My children died. They'll not help you.

Girl I'm sorry.

Woman Your "sorry" will not help you.

Girl What then? What! You say I must repay a debt. Must you pull down the whole of history on to me? Things that happened before I was born. Your broken windows are not my fault.

The Man enters

We are moving place.

Woman Again?

The Man blindfolds the Girl

The Lights fade

SCENE 9

The dusty road

Soldier One and Soldier Two are nestled up together. They have their knapsacks with them

Soldier Two wakes and looks around for several moments. He rubs his eyes a lot and yawns. He shakes Soldier One

Soldier Two Come on, come on …

Soldier One Leave off …

Soldier Two You must … Come on …

Soldier One All right. Oooh. All right. (*Still half asleep*) Here I am.

Soldier Two Here. But where is here?

Soldier One Bed. Bloody hard bed.

Soldier Two No bed.

Soldier One Like bloody baked clay.

Soldier Two Open your eyes.

Soldier One does so and groans

See.

Soldier One Clay. Red clay. Where's the bed? Where's the walls? What happened? And where the hell were you? I got the goats, took them home, then his folks started treating me like a king. Reckon I could've had the daughter for the asking. Wait … (*He fumbles in his pocket and takes out money*) That's real enough. He gave me the money for the — melon patch … He said a melon patch. Can you see a melon patch?

Soldier Two There is no melon patch.

Soldier One So — last night — made a deal — got given a bed. Now you're here and we're sitting in the middle of a bloody dustbowl. I'm going back to sleep.

Soldier Two You cannot.

Soldier One It'll sort itself out with a sleep. We're having a bad dream. If we go back to sleep things'll get back to normal. But the money. That's real enough. Let's be logical about this. I've got the money, so I must've been there. Then we ended up here. All we need to do is figure out what happened in between. Something I've forgotten. What have I forgotten? No. Ah. Right. Got it. *Why* did I forget it? I *wanted* to forget it, that's why I forgot it. But it's tucked away somewhere, in some little corner of my head, waiting to be remembered.

Soldier Two Hmm ... You *wanted* to forget.

Soldier One Original, eh?

Soldier Two Most. An excellent theory. You could put it in a book. The mind decided to protect itself. By forgetting.

Soldier One Bet they never taught you *that* in school.

Soldier Two But you must prove it.

Soldier One Prove it?

Soldier Two Scientifically. At the moment it is still a hypothesis.

Soldier One Don't show off.

Soldier Two An idea. It's an idea.

Soldier One Damn good one.

Soldier Two But you have to prove it.

Soldier One Let's find some breakfast first. Got anything?

They rummage through their knapsacks

Soldier Two (*producing a piece of hard cheese*) A piece of hard cheese.

Soldier One (*producing a bit of sausage*) Bit of sausage.

Soldier Two (*producing a piece of dry bread*) Dry bread.

Soldier One That'll do.

They eat in silence for a while

Soldier Two So. The worst thing that may have happened. So bad you made yourself forget it. Did you kill them?

Soldier One That's not so bad. We've been killing people in droves for the last three years.

Soldier Two That was war.

Soldier One Killing is killing.

Soldier Two For your country?

Soldier One Hmm. There's a question to be asked there. Can't quite get it. But it'll come. I feel my head is expanding. Does it look like it's expanding?

Soldier Two It seems the usual shape.

Soldier One Like there's bits of brain multiplying. Something really terrible I did. Imagine. Rape ... No, of course, that's just war again.

Soldier Two Maybe ... You didn't do anything.

Soldier One That's not terrible.

Soldier Two When the ones they called the bastards came in the night.

Soldier One Did they?

Soldier Two They crept in by the moonlight. And made the father rape the daughter. The son the mother. Then kill each other.

Soldier One Did they? I never did *that*, war or no war.

Soldier Two But what you did ... What you did was — you stayed in the dark and held your breath. Didn't come to their help. Saved your own skin. Waited till it was all over. Then stepped over the bodies and headed off into the night. Walked and walked. Fell down here. Slept.

Soldier One No. No.

Soldier Two Maybe.

Soldier One Forget it.

Soldier Two And if you did, your theory would be corr ——

Soldier One I refuse to believe I cou ——

Soldier Two Are you afraid of what you mi ——

Soldier One Leave off or I'll ——

Soldier Two You don't want to remember wha ——

Soldier One Shut it or I ——

Soldier Two Is it coming to the surface, all the ——

Soldier One Shut your gob! (*He hits Soldier Two*) You brought that on yourself. You're not meant to do it like that. Don't you understand? If someone's been trying to forget something, something terrible, you don't go on at them. You lay them down on a couch and talk gentle. Coax them. In their own time. Start prodding and bullying, you'll get a smack in the mouth. Did I hurt you?

Soldier Two No more than a feather.

Soldier One That's war, eh? Toughens you up.

Soldier Two I missed you.

Soldier One Me too. Let's find the gun. I sold one of them. Thought you'd buggered off, so I sold it. And we need a gun. He buried it in the melon patch.

Soldier Two No melon patch.

Soldier One (*crawling around, feeling the ground*) It would need to be soft earth. If we find soft earth ...

Soldier Two (*feeling the ground*) Packed solid.

Soldier One We need a method. In a straight line, together.

They line up on their hands and knees, side by side. They crawl forward, feeling the ground. They do this for a while

Soldier Two Ah-ha! (*He holds up a melon pip*) Pip of the melon?
Soldier One Pip, eh! From a melon! Could be.
Soldier Two Dig away.

They dig

The Lights fade

SCENE 10

A room in a ruined castle

The Girl, the Woman and the Man are on stage. The Girl is blindfolded. The Man is looking through the Girl's wallet. During the following he takes a newspaper cutting from the wallet

Girl Are we still in the city?
Man That would be telling.
Woman I'm happy to be away from the city.
Man Shut that.
Woman There's no harm.
Man You are too soft.
Woman I don't cry for my children.
Man Everyone's children died.
Girl How did they die?
Man How does anything die?
Girl I mean — by chance or ——
Man All right …

The Man takes the Girl's blindfold off. He shows the Girl the newspaper cutting taken from her wallet

That man?
Girl My father.
Man (*showing the cutting to the Woman*) Her father. And he's shaking the hand of the other man. Look at the other man.
Woman (*looking at the cutting*) Yes.
Man Her father shakes the hand of his president. How important he looks. They are smiling at the camera. Beautiful suits. Standing on the steps. Her price is rising. I'm thinking about ears.
Woman That goes too far. She is a foolish child, not ——
Man A fool to come here. Didn't they warn you? You should have stayed on the coast. In a tourist compound. Discothèques. Waiters.
Girl I've no interest in that.

Man (*to the Woman*) Read about her father. What he sells.
Woman We must not be cruel.
Man Chemicals. (*To the Girl*) Does he have religion, your father? What does it say? "An ear for an ear"?
Woman Not her.
Man Too soft. (*To the Girl*) Look at those walls. That is not water seeping out of the stones. It is blood. Kings built this place, high on the mountain, deep in the rock. Chambers like this. They tortured our heroes. Before the Great Change. Before your great-grandfather ran away. And now your father shakes the hand of his president. Signs contracts. Sends chemicals to poison children. Not the tourists on the coast. You should have taken the advice of the brochures. You would have been safe. (*He takes out a knife*) Your father is not cruel by nature. I know that. We too are not. If we have to cut off your ear and send it to your father, that is merely history unwinding.

The Lights fade

SCENE 11

The dusty road

Soldier One is digging with his hands. Soldier Two is writing in his notebook

Soldier Two How does this sound? (*Reading*) "It is the travelling, not the arriving, that counts."
Soldier One Rubbish.
Soldier Two It is a great saying, in my own country. Now I translate it. Perhaps "is significant" would be better. "It is the travelling that is significant, not the arriving."
Soldier One It's like saying, "just keep digging, even if there's nothing to dig for." Look at my hands. Nothing significant there, just bleeding fingers.
Soldier Two It is about life.
Soldier One Life's about getting down to the gun. When some bunch of roughnecks set on us we'll need that gun. Without that gun we'll not be arriving anywhere.
Soldier Two (*reading*) "Travelling light is less easy once affection is involved."
Soldier One I'll go along with that.

Two Archaeologists enter. They have shiny backpacks. Archaeologist One carries a coolbag

Archaeologist One Hey! You two!

Soldiers One and Two stop digging and look

Archaeologist Two What are you doing?
Soldier One Burying a bone. His name's Rover and I'm Rex. (*He resumes digging*)
Archaeologist One Well you'll have to stop.
Soldier One (*digging*) It's a free country.
Archaeologist One This is an authorized site.
Soldier One (*digging*) Here's something.
Soldier Two (*reading*) "The only certainty is uncertainty."
Soldier One Wrong. It's certainly a gun.
Archaeologist One (*producing a document*) See. Site of special archaeological interest. Authorized permit to dig. Ministry of Heritage.

Soldier One unearths his gun and lifts it out of the cavity

Soldier One There you are.
Archaeologist Two That is government property. (*He takes the gun*)
Soldier One That is my gun.
Archaeologist One Nonsense. You took it out of the ground.
Archaeologist Two We saw you.
Archaeologist One Technically, that was theft.
Soldier Two A man is not able to steal his own gun.
Archaeologist One (*aside, to Archaeologist Two*) Drugs. They'll be from that bunch of protesters back there.
Archaeologist Two We'll keep our distance. Handle them gently. (*To Soldiers One and Two*) I think you may have got the wrong place, gentlemen.
Soldier Two The wrong place?
Archaeologist Two The road protest is at the other end of the valley.
Soldier Two Road what?
Archaeologist Two We're not here to damage nature. We're here to bring the past back. To track down the glories that have been sleeping beneath us through the ages.
Archaeologist One We'd never dream of running a road through a burial-site.
Soldier One (*aside to Soldier Two*) They've probably escaped from a loony bin. We'd better humour them. (*To the Archaeologists*) We lost our way. Sorry if we were any bother.
Archaeologist Two Not at all. So. If you walk for about an hour or so in that direction — (*he points*) you'll be home and dry,
Soldier One (*aside to Soldier Two*) Can't leave without the gun.
Soldier Two (*to Archaeologist One*) Foot is bad. Need to rest it.

Soldier One We'll just sit here. Till he's feeling better.

Archaeologist One Well, actually — (*he produces a chart and looks at it*) you can't sit *just* there.

Soldier One I can bloody well … I mean, oh really, why not?

Archaeologist One That's where — if our deductions are correct — the royal wives are buried.

Soldier One Ah. Of course. The royal wives.

Archaeologist One So — if you wish to sit …

Soldier One With your permission, of course …

Archaeologist One You could sit — (*he points*) over there.

Soldier Two That would be a *nice* place to sit.

Soldier One (*aside to Soldier Two*) What did I say? Barking. (*To the Archaologists*) We'd *adore* to sit there. We can't wait to sit there.

Archaeologist Two (*aside to Archaeologist One*) Hear that? Out of their heads on something.

The Soldiers shift position

Archaeologist One Comfy?

Soldier One Ever so.

Archaeologist One Terrific. Now. The royal wives are located somewhere here … (*Aside*) They're from the road protest, no doubt about it … (*To the Soldiers*) Yes. See how the sun picks out the ridges running there, and there … (*Aside*) Drugged up to the eyeballs. (*To the Soldiers*) Good. Our task is to take a small vertical earth-sample … (*Aside*) Just behave normally until we can get the police here. (*To the Soldiers*) So. About one metre … (*Aside*) And if they mention the gun don't provoke them. (*To the Soldiers*) Then we'll take the sample back to the lab and examine it.

The Archaeologists produce a sieve, a magnifying glass and a little brush from their backpacks. One of them dusts the ground with the brush

Soldier Two Why would they want the royal wives?

Soldier One No, no, there aren't any royal wives. Who'd stick royal wives in a place like this?

Soldier Two When there was the Great Change, they gunned them all down in a cellar. Then they threw them down a mineshaft.

Soldier One The royal wives?

Soldier Two The lot. The royal dogs went in as well.

Soldier One That's a rotten trick.

Archaeologist One (*holding up a fragment*) Bingo! Now this fragment is like the fragment that was discovered last year (*he points*) — over there. Identical. I'd say.

Archaeologist Two What was over there?
Archaeologist One The royal lavatory.
Archaeologist Two Did they have lavatories?
Archaeologist One Well, not lavatories as we'd know them. No flushing.
Archaeologist Two So they lost this fragment down the pan, so to speak?
Archaeologist One Don't make jokes, we're talking about dead royalty. This fragment would have belonged to a servant. It's pewter. But this it indicates that there was activity here.
Soldier Two We should've hung on to that gun. Bashed them over the head and made a run for it.

Archaeologist One takes a bottle of mineral water out of the coolbag. The Archaeologists drink

Archaeologist Two I needed that.
Archaeologist One Just what the doctor ordered.
Soldier One That'll be their medication. Calms them down.
Soldier Two It reminds me of my thirst.

Archaeologist One crosses to them

Soldier One If he offers, say no — but be polite.
Archaeologist One Would you care to ——
Soldier One We're fine.
Archaeologist One Wouldn't want our guests to suffer.
Soldier One You are very gracious.
Archaeologist One Cool you down. Feel the bottle.
Soldier Two (*taking the bottle*) Oooh.
Archaeologist One See
Soldier Two So cold.
Soldier One In this heat?
Archaeologist One Coolbag.
Soldier One Coolbag?
Soldier Two "Coolbag". (*He writes in his notebook*)
Soldier One (*looking at the bottle*) This — coolbag … What does it do?
Archaeologist One It keeps the temperature down, of course.
Soldier One I had a temperature on my tenth birthday.
Soldier Two (*placing the bottle on his forehead*) Aah.
Soldier One My mother placed cold flannels on my body. Give us a go. (*He takes the bottle and places it on his forehead*)
Soldier Two There was a park near my house. On hot days I'd sit by the fountain and put my fingers in the water. Flick it over my face.
Archaeologist One So — what happened?

Soldier Two When?
Archaeologist One You clearly came from a good family. I — don't get me
wrong — I don't disapprove of your way of life …
Soldier Two Nor we yours.
Archaeologist One You seem perfectly — decent …
Soldier Two And we feel very — secure — in your company.
Archaeologist One But — you come from — normal — homes?
Soldier Two As no doubt yourself.
Archaeologist One So — why this life?
Soldier One What other life is there?
Archaeologist One Don't you want clean white sheets? Have a table with
flowers in a vase? A shelf of books?
Soldier One That's where I'm heading. Him too. When we hit the north.
Archaeologist Going back to settle down?
Soldier One You bet.
Archaeologist One Give me your hand.

Archaeologist One shakes Soldier One's hand firmly

You've made my day.
Soldier One Really. May I — ask you something?
Archaeologist One Fire away.
Soldier One Will you ever — get better?
Archaeologist One It's my philosophy. "Every day, in every way, I will get
better and better."
Soldier One That's the spirit. (*To Soldier Two*) He wants to get better.
Archaeologist One Don't we all?
Soldier Two However, *we* are not off our hea ——
Soldier One Hurrumph!
Archaeologist One I study and study. I keep up with all the latest techniques.
Did you know that there's now a method of scanning the foundations of a
site, and building up a three-dimensional image of how it once was? Isn't
that fantastic? I'm going on a course. There's new things coming to light
every day. And the stuff that's coming out of the ground. More and more
of it. There's something — spiritual about it, don't you think? Not just out
of the ground, but the ice and the water, too. Cleopatra's palace floats up
to us from the floor of the delta. Mummified bodies in the peat bogs. You
can open their stomachs and find out what their last meal was. A four
hundred year-old banana, preserved in the remains of a rubbish tip. A
glacier slowly delivers a sheep-driver up, a thousand years old and fresh
as a new born baby. In fact, sometimes I think that it's something to do with
the age we're living in. The Earth giving birth to the past — pushing it up
through her surface, sending it back to us. What for I'm not sure.

Soldier One To remind us.
Archaeologist One Eh?
Soldier One To remind us of what went before. Not just stories. Things we
can touch. To let us know that it's still with us. Where did I get that from?
(*To SoldierTwo*) What shape is my head?
Soldier Two The same.
Soldier One It feels all fizzy inside. Like a bottle of lemonade about to pop.
Archaeologist One You know my dream? To discover the library at
Alexandria.
Soldier Two The library at Alexandria.
Archaeologist One Isn't that a beautiful thought?
Soldier Two The library at Alexandria.

A silence

Soldier One They didn't even tell me there *was* one. But I got along without
it. Why didn't they tell me? They told you there was an enemy. Bang!
Bang!
Archaeologist One Now don't get over-excited.
Soldier One Be a sport. Give the gun back. Or (*he holds on to the bottle*) …
we won't let you have this. It's getting dark. You could do it on the sly.
You'll be needing your medication, won't you?
Archaeologist One Medication?
Soldier One Fair swap. Give gun, get medication.
Archaeologist One It's a bottle of water.
Soldier One Water! Ha ha! Good try.
Archaeologist One Oh dear. I thought you'd reformed.
Archaeologist Two (*calling*) They're here.
Archaeologist One Listen. If I tell the cops you're heading home …
Soldier One We are.
Archaeologist One Yes, but even if you're not, just pretend that
you're ——
Soldier One You saying I'm a liar?
Archaeologist One Keep calm, don't ——
Soldier One Where d'you think we're going? And we need that gun to get
us through. There's all sorts of nutters about.
Soldier Two That was a bad choice of word.

A person from the Militia enters

Militia Trouble here?
Archaeologist Two Attempted theft. Hindrance of work. Verbal threats.
Archaeologist One They didn't mean any ——

Militia That's three bookable offences.
Archaeologist Two Road protesters.
Militia They're for the cooler. (*To the Soldiers*) OK. On your feet.
Soldier One They took our gun.
Archaeologist Two They were digging it up.
Soldier One The goatboy buried it. I slept in his parents' bed. They didn't like guns in the house and he buried it in the melon patch. We were getting it back.
Militia So where's the melons?
Soldier One (*fishing in his pocket and producing the seed*) That's a melon-seed. It was over there.
Archaeologist One Melon-seed! Evidence of cultivation.
Militia Step with me, gentlemen.
Soldier One We'll step nowhere with you.
Militia (*drawing his pistol*) Placing bets?
Soldier One What a beauty.
Militia Keep your distance.
Soldier One I was admiring the design.
Archaeologist One Gun mad.
Soldier One (*aside, to Militia*) They're the mad ones. They brush the mud. We've been keeping an eye on them. You should get them back to their bin. They shouldn't be allowed to roam.
Militia OK, OK. (*To the Soldiers*) Now, on the double. Now! Hands in the air! Go!
Archaeologist One Don't be too harsh with them.

The Militia person marches the Soldiers towards the exit

Soldier One (*calling*) The things rising to the surface. Are they coming back to tell us we've failed? What we've thrown away? What we've lost?
Archaeologist One I don't know, I don't know.

The Militia person, Soldier One and Soldier Two exit

Archaeologist Two Let's classify this rifle.
Archaeologist One (*calling to the Soldiers*) Good luck!
Soldier One (*off*) Say hallo to the royal wives.
Soldier Two (*off*) Divorced, beheaded, died, divorced, beheaded, survived.
Archaeologist One (*calling*) Richard Of York Gave Battle In Vain.

The Lights fade

The interval is optional. If an interval is being taken, it should be at this point

ACT II
Scene 1

A hospital

The Girl is on stage. She is reading the notebook. She has a bandage around her head

Girl (*reading*) "They tell me that I am right to learn this language. That it is the language of the future. Of trade and industry. And that I will prosper under it. It is a language I love, certainly. In particular, because I can now read the poet in his own tongue. But does this mean that I will forget my own poets? And what if poets' language is the language of the future? What happens to the other languages? How they tell the world differently. I write the words 'hope', but in my own tongue it has other flavours. What if my own tongue dies for lack of usage? A variety of hope will have died with it."

The Lights fade

Scene 2

A prison cell

Soldier One and Soldier Two are in the cell. In the darkness of a far corner a Prisoner sits chained, as yet not visible to the audience

Soldier One is reading the walls with his hands. Soldier Two has his ear to the floor

Soldier One (*reading*) "Mother remember me." "My name is" ... "My name is" ... "Kilroy was here." This prison wall is becoming very tedious. Kilroy. Mother.
Soldier Two This prison floor is definitely hollow.
Soldier One "My name is" ... Now here's a better one: "Education is dead and so are lots of elephants."
Soldier Two No sound. But hollow. (*He scrabbles around on the floor, finds a rusty nail and pokes at the wall with it*) Not granite, anyway. Granite'd be useless. This is powdery. That's a good sign.

Soldier One Isn't that remarkable?

Soldier Two Yes. If I was building a prison I'd use granite. Only thing shifts granite is dynamite.

Soldier One I mean elephants.

Soldier Two I've seen elephants. One was pulling a house along. The house was on a raft on a river. The elephant was on the riverbank. Huge house. More a mansion. Work. (*He scratches more*)

Soldier One A house. What have elephants and houses to do with each other?

Soldier Two Or nails and freedom.

Soldier One Or elephants and education.

Soldier Two Or you and me.

Soldier One Or cats' paws and the sea.

Soldier Two stops scratching and grunts interrogatively. He puts the nail down

Soldier One Put them together.

Soldier Two Cats hate the sea. Dogs love the water. Not cats.

Soldier One Something brings them together.

Soldier Two Never.

Soldier One Mist.

Soldier Two Mist?

Soldier One Have a go.

Soldier Two This is a waste of time. Here's another nail. Get scratching.

Soldier One It goes like this — let me get it right — yes ... "The mist crept in from the sea on little cats' paws."

Soldier Two Did it?

Soldier One Don't you get it?

Soldier Two Get what?

Soldier One Without the mist, you'd never get the sea and cats together. Now you'll not think of the mist coming in from the sea the same. Ever again.

Soldier Two If we don't get out of here we'll never get to the sea. Or any place else. Soft stone, hollow below. It's a risk. A way out, or a torture chamber.

There are the sounds of bolts and locks

Soldier One Look casual.

A Guard enters

Guard (*to Soldier Two*) You first.

Soldier Two What for?
Guard You'll discover.
Soldier One I'll come too.
Guard You'll wait.
Soldier One We never part. We're a team.
Guard (*picking up the nail*) Been scratching, eh?
Soldier Two My name.
Guard Very wise.
Soldier Two You think?
Guard Saves us a lot of bother.
Soldier Two How?
Guard Records get lost. When they come for the body we don't know who it was. If they scratch a name, then the relatives can confirm.
Soldier Two Very convenient.
Guard So by all means, use the nail. Add a bit of poetry, too.
Soldier Two Some do.
Guard The relatives like that. It comforts them, to think that, even as death approached, their child had a sensitive soul. Mind you, most of it's sentimental rubbish. Like you get on gravestones. A lack of dignity. Quotations are best, from the great poets. You can't go wrong with a quotation, dedicated to your Ma. Off we go.
Soldier Two Where?
Guard To get scratched.
Soldier Two I'd rather not.
Guard You get double rations after. To build you up.
Soldier Two Could we skip it?
Guard The first time's quite gentle.

Soldier Two and the Guard exit

Soldier One sits and listens for a moment. He fishes in his pocket and brings out a bit of dried bread and considers it. He takes a nibble and chews

Soldier One Mouldy. (*He looks at the bread*) All right. Lamb cutlet. (*He chews again*) Not bad. Fish pie. (*He chews*) Hmm. Roasted duck with a light chestnut glaze and stuffed with baby quails marinated in honey and orange. (*He chews. It doesn't work this time*)
Prisoner An onion.

Soldier One peers across the cell

Soldier One Who's that? Come out of the shadows.
Prisoner A bar of chocolate.

Soldier One Stop mucking about. Who are you? They didn't say we'd be sharing.

Prisoner A carton of milk.

Soldier One I'm coming over. No funny business, I'm a fighting man. (*He feels his way towards the Prisoner*)

Prisoner A loaf of bread.

Soldier One Keep going.

Prisoner My thesis on "The Rights of Man".

Soldier One Doesn't sound very edible. Nearly there. Got you. (*He touches the chains*) What's this?

The Prisoner shifts into the light

That can't be very comfortable.

Prisoner You get used to it.

Soldier One Why didn't you announce yourself?

Prisoner I sleep a lot. There were voices, but I thought it was my dream. Then the talk of roasted duck ...

Soldier One The roasted duck didn't work. I was pushing my luck.

Prisoner So I thought it was them.

Soldier One With roasted duck?

Prisoner It's almost worse than the scratching. They come and whisper food.

Soldier One Why?

Prisoner I'm on hunger strike. They whisper meals to me. Whole menus, ten-course banquets with all the trimmings. You tell yourself it's just words, but the belly has its own mind. It aches and aches. I think of my dead comrades, crushed by the tanks, bleeding in the square, in the hope that grief will abolish hunger. It doesn't. Then I feel ashamed, that I should use grief for my friends to try and stop the pangs.

Soldier One The best meal I ever had, it was in the trenches. A bit of boiled mutton and onion gravy. I can taste it now. I can feel the gravy dribbling down my chops. That was just after I'd seen my two lovely brothers blown to smithereens in front of me. The belly doesn't know grief. It just sits down there, waiting for the next offering. Lurks there, all greedy. We're its servants. So don't feel bad.

Soldier Two screams, off

My pal.

Another scream

And I could still eat a horse.

Another scream

Prisoner So then I try to remember who I really am.
Soldier One Who's that?
Prisoner I start with the onion.
Soldier One Now wait. Look — whatever they've done — this place — the menus, the chains … You have to keep telling yourself that you are *not a vegetable!*
Prisoner No, no, the onion was in the plastic bag.
Soldier One Ah.
Prisoner Along with the milk and the chocolate. And my thesis on "The Rights of Man".
Soldier One And that's you?
Prisoner That's who I was. When the ranks came into the square. I'm told there was a photograph in the newspapers. Worldwide. You saw it?
Soldier One I've been a bit tied up the last few years. Not much time for the papers.
Prisoner You must've seen it.
Soldier One Sorry.
Prisoner In my shirtsleeves. Standing with the plastic bag in front of the tank. In the square.
Soldier One Sounds impressive, but it doesn't ring a bell. But I'm sure ——
Prisoner Never mind.
Soldier One Don't let it depress you. I was never one for the papers. Too gloomy-doomy. But I'm sure the rest of the world saw you.

The Guard and Soldier Two enter. Soldier Two is in a bad way

Soldier One moves away from the Prisoner

Guard You'd do best not to talk to that one.
Soldier One Those menus are very cruel.
Guard He's getting the full state banquet tomorrow.
Soldier One (*to Soldier Two*) Tell me.
Soldier Two Not good.
Soldier One (*to the Guard*) Let's get it over with.
Guard You're eager.
Soldier One Waiting's the worst.
Guard You're tomorrow.
Soldier One Couldn't you just squeeze me in?
Guard I've got a life, you know. Kids to be collected from school. Lawn to mow. Second job.
Soldier One Second job? You must get very tired.

Guard We've not been paid for three months.
Soldier One That's an outrage.
Guard So what with school fees, gas bills ...
Soldier One Terrible.
Guard It's my wife's birthday. I can't even afford a present for her.
Soldier One Awful.
Guard I might even need to take a third job. So I can't fit you in tonight.
Soldier One I'd rather not sleep on it.
Guard Oh, you won't sleep.
Soldier One And where's his double-rations?
Guard The canteen staff have gone on strike.

The Guard exits

Soldier Two moans

Soldier One Yes, yes ... (*He cradles Soldier Two*) But we have a new friend.
Soldier Two (*in pain*) Where — did — he — come — from?
Soldier One From the shadows.

Soldier Two moans

I know, I know ... (*He rocks Soldier Two*) He did something very brave.
There, there. It all began with an onion and the rights of man.
Soldier Two Is this the end?
Soldier One The end? After all we've been through?
Soldier Two If I'd not gone after those goats ...
Soldier One Don't think about it.
Soldier Two Translating poetry in that wretched notebook. What was the
use of that?
Soldier One Wait! Of course! (*He bangs on the cell door*) Hey! Hey!
Soldier Two Poetry!
Soldier One (*calling*) Hey! I've remembered something! (*To Soldier Two*)
Hope springs eternal? Specially when it rhymes.

The Guard enters

Guard I'm off duty.
Soldier One I was considering your wife's birthday.
Guard That was very thoughtful.
Soldier One Lack of present.
Guard It's a problem.
Soldier One Problem solved.
Guard Meaning?

Soldier One Poem.
Guard Poem?
Soldier One My friend is a writer. Give her a love poem.
Guard What a tender thought.
Soldier One Tell her it came out of your own head.
Guard (*to Soldier Two*) You up to it?
Soldier Two After what you did to me?
Soldier One (*whispering to Soldier Two*) Forget that. We can do a *deal!*
Guard No whispering.
Soldier One (*to the Guard*) I'm bringing him round to the idea. (*Whispering*) Poem for him, freedom for us. Get it?
Soldier Two Got it. (*He writes in his notebook during the following*)
Soldier One (*to the Guard*) Settled. Tomorrow morning. For free.
Guard Nothing comes for free.
Soldier One A poem. How love *frees* the soul. How it *opens the prison door* of the heart. How it *unbolts the locks of the* human spirit.
Guard I'm getting the drift.
Soldier One Two human spirits in this case.
Guard The poem had better be good.
Soldier One All original work.
Guard No crap.
Soldier One It'll bring tears to her eyes.
Guard Crack of dawn then. And not a word to our friend in the corner. And make sure it rhymes.

The Guard exits

Soldier One (*to Soldier Two*) How's it going?
Soldier Two "When life and all its echoes fade away,
          And this brief melody has come to rest,
          Of each and every note that I have heard
          Your voice will linger on forever blessed."
Soldier One No, no, he wants something *original*.
Soldier Two I just made it up.
Soldier One You made that up?
Soldier Two I'm not sure about "rest" and "blessed".
Soldier One It's far too good for that shit to give his wife. You really made it up?
Soldier Two It is easy. You just go tee-tum, tee-tum.
Soldier One Will you write me a poem one day?
Soldier Two When we get to the north.
Soldier One And we'll get there. We're out of here tomorrow. First light.
Soldier Two (*nodding towards the Prisoner*) Him too?
Soldier One Course not.

Soldier Two Why not?

Soldier One He's political, we're just passing trash. No-one'll notice our absence.

Soldier Two It seems somehow fair.

Soldier One And he's be a liability. His picture's been in the papers, worldwide.

They peer across towards the Prisoner

Is he awake?

Soldier Two Let's explain the position. We can't just leave him.

Soldier One You awake?

Prisoner It all seems the same.

Soldier One I'm coming over. (*He crawls across to the Prisoner*) We're — being transferred tomorrow. But here's something … (*He holds up the nail*) I've made a start on the floor over there.

Prisoner Unpick the locks.

Soldier One Locks?

Prisoner (*holding up his chains*) With the nail. Here. When he comes tomorrow, we could smash his head with these. Make a break.

Soldier One Well — no …

Prisoner We've nothing to lose.

Soldier One It — wouldn't be wise. Tell you what. I'll hang on to the nail. Then I'll leave it for you, just as we're going. You settle down now. (*He crawls back to Soldier Two*)

Soldier Two How did he take it?

Soldier One Very sympathetic. I told him he'd be a liability. He found our point of view entirely acceptable.

Soldier Two But is it acceptable to us?

Soldier One If a person has a point of view, then it's bound to be acceptable to them. You wouldn't expect a person to have a point of view they didn't accept, would you? I mean if my point of view was: "Mankind are no better than rats in sewers", then that would be acceptable to me. I wouldn't secretly be thinking: "That's an unacceptable point of view, and that Mankind are angels in glory." Because then *that* would be my point of view. (*Pause*) What nonsense. How simple-minded. (*Pause*) How do I know that? (*Pause*) Anyway, to plough on, why can't I have two points of view at the same time? Rats and angels. Oooh, my head hurts. Rats and angels. It doesn't have to be "either-or". It can be "and-also". And also — how do I know this? — everyone else knows it. Has known it. But me. Why didn't they tell me? My head feels like it's going to burst. Everything is dissolving. The walls of this place. Like glass. I can see the stars. I could step through. "Iron bars do not a prison make." Who said that? Someone must have said it because I put inverted commas around it. *Why can't I have an original thought?*

The Lights fade

Scene 3

A press conference in a hotel

The Girl listens to an unheard question and then answers

Girl No. No, I don't think it meant my father did not love me. Well … He was in a difficult position. And how was he to know that it was *my* ear? Listen, it could have been anyone's ear. As I said, he was in a difficult position — and the government has a very strict policy. …Yes, of course he must have known the risk, the danger to me. … Yes, I do still love him. Well, they didn't kill me, did they? … No, I don't think I do hate them. … I said I don't think I … No, I know I don't hate them. If you want to know, I think I was naïve and foolish to go there, knowing the risks. … No, I wouldn't call them fanatics, I wouldn't — will not — use that word. … Of course, but terrible things have happened there, things I'd no idea of, babies dying — no food. … Now? Well … Go home. … No, not straight away, I want to collect my thoughts — discover what my thoughts are. I'm not sure what I've learned, maybe I'll discover that before I go home. Oh yes, I'll tell you what kept me going. (*She produces the notebook and reads*)
　　"Cowards die many times before their deaths;
　　The valiant never taste death but once.
　　Of all the wonders that I yet have heard,
　　It seems to me most strange that men should fear,
　　Seeing that death, a necessary end,
　　Will come when it will come."
Actually, that's what I think. Of course I can think someone else's thought. Isn't that what we do all the time? Think other people's thoughts and think they are our own?

The Lights fade

Scene 4

Open countryside. Dusk

Soldier One and Soldier Two are onstage

Soldier Two Steady

Soldier One On my feet.
Soldier Two Here we are.
Soldier One Where?
Soldier Two Stepped outside. See?
Soldier One (*looking around*) Where's the stone? Where's the nail? Where's the chap with the plastic bag? What the hell is plastic? Why can't I stop asking questions?
Soldier Two Whatever happened, it worked. Walls to glass. Glass dissolved.
Soldier One There's the sky.
Soldier Two And a river.
Soldier One And trees.
Soldier Two Thank you.
Soldier One I didn't do a thing. Wait a minute — did I leave him the nail?
Soldier Two Who?
Soldier One Who? *Who?*
Soldier Two Oh, yes — maybe I do rem ——
Soldier One You've *forgotten* him?
Soldier Two It seems so long ago.
Soldier One He could've been our son.
Soldier Two We are two men.
Soldier One Why can't two men have a son? Eh? Why not? He could've been. He stood in shirt sleeves in a square, with "The Rights of Man" and an onion. In front of a tank. And we didn't move a muscle to save him.
Soldier Two We were not there.
Soldier One He wanted me to use the nail to pick the lock.
Soldier Two Then you lied to me. And it was not me who refused his request.
Soldier One (*hitting Soldier Two*) Bastard! Bastard!

A long pause

I think I'm sorry.
Soldier Two I think I forgive you.

A pause

Soldier One Shall we go?
Soldier Two Yes. Let's go.
Soldier One Oh. Oh.
Soldier Two Speak out.
Soldier One Somewhere beautiful. Let's go somewhere beautiful. Cherry blossoms in an orchard. Music drifting out into the garden. I only ever had a back yard, and it faced north; nothing grew.
Soldier Two Map and compass.

They rummage in their pockets and produce the map and the compass

Soldier One Did I hurt you?
Soldier Two Does it matter?
Soldier One "Deliberate cruelty is not acceptable." There I go again. But it's true, even if I didn't say it.
Soldier Two You did say it.
Soldier One Someone got there before me.
Soldier Two And it is not acceptable. Now, the map ... (*He looks at the map*)
Soldier One But what about casual cruelty?
Soldier Two We're making headway.
Soldier One Is that acceptable?
Soldier Two (*referring to the map*) Why does it always get bigger? Those mountain ranges — were they there before?
Soldier One How many men did I bayonet?
Soldier Two And that river delta. How can we cross that?
Soldier One Deliberate or casual? Or both?
Soldier Two And there's something bothering me.
Soldier One Both.
Soldier Two *I said*, something is bothering me.

Soldier One grunts interrogatively

It was my gun we sold, but you kept the money.
Soldier One We're a team.
Soldier Two We take half each.
Soldier One Don't you trust me?
Soldier Two Half.
Soldier One Some trust. (*He produces the money and hands Soldier Two half of it*) Go on, count it.
Soldier Two (*handing it back*) It was just to see.
Soldier One And I passed the test?
Soldier Two We both passed the test.
Soldier One Brothers at last.
Soldier Two Under the moon.

They look up

Soldier One Night happens very quickly round here.
Soldier Two (*pointing to the map*) If my calculations are correct, we're —
here.
Soldier One And we started out ... ?
Soldier Two There.

Soldier One I was by the road. Cooking up. A lifetime ago.
Soldier Two And I came by.
Soldier One It had to happen like that. Like the moon. (*He lies down and looks up*) Some things never change. People will be looking at the moon when you and I are …

Soldier Two takes out his notebook and writes

Read to me.
Soldier Two (*reading*) "My friend is looking at the moon."
Soldier One So I'm in there. One day someone will find that. I'll be quoted. It'll be published. I'll become an exam question.
Soldier Two Sssh.

Soldier One grunts interrogatively

Someone. (*He puts his notebook away*)

They listen and watch

No. The light of the moon. It cast a shadow.

They lie and look at the moon

       "That very time I saw — but thou couldst not —
       Flying between the cold moon and the earth
       Cupid all armed."
Soldier One Cupid, eh? Come here.

They curl up on the ground, spoon-fashion

I wonder where we'll be tomorrow.
Soldier Two On the moon.
Soldier One Oh yes?
Soldier Two It'll happen. Anything can happen.
Soldier One How come?
Soldier Two I just imagined it. My foot on the moon. And it's …

They sleep

The Lights fade

SCENE 5

A dark cave

The Girl and a Tour Guide with a torch are in the cave

Girl (*looking at the floor*) Twenty-one centimetres?
Guide Twenty-one.
Girl That's a small footprint.
Guide A child, perhaps.
Girl A child? In such a deep cave?
Guide You know what children are like. They go into nooks and crannies. Make dens. Look how we're having to crouch. A cave like this would be a joy for a child. (*Calling*) Can those at the back move forward. It's important that the party stays close to me. These caves go on for miles, it is easy to get lost.
Girl I'd not want a child of mine down here alone.
Guide (*shining the torch upwards*) He had a light with him.
Girl How's that?
Guide See. On the ceiling. Those grubby patches. Charcoal marks. He would have rubbed off the charcoal on the ceiling to revive the torch. We can't be sure. But the footprints on the floor and the marks on the ceiling might be connected.
Girl What were his parents thinking of?
Guide Through radiocarbon dating, the torchmarks above the footprints are estimated to be twenty-six thousand years old.
Girl Didn't they care?
Guide And so if the footprint and the torchmarks are connected they ——
Girl What sort of thoughts did people have then?
Guide See how the soil is still damp. The temperature is constant in a place like this. If left undisturbed the soil would retain its moisture, the print would remain fresh.
Girl A child came down here, twenty-six thousand years ago, alone, with a torch …
Guide And some food. See that crack in the wall. That's where the bit of bone was found. He'd brought a snack with him.
Girl Came down and made his den here one afternoon.
Guide While his parents were in the upper caves, painting the animals on the walls. Those lions, mammoths.
Girl What was he thinking?
Guide That we'll never know. But there is his footprint. Still fresh.

The Lights fade

SCENE 6

The same setting as Act II Scene 4

Soldier One is alone and asleep. He wakes up suddenly and scrabbles around in the moonlight, looking for Soldier Two

Soldier One Gone! Gone! (*He cries for a moment*) Nothing but the moon. (*Calling out*) Well, rot you! Hope you're dead! I don't want the money! (*He produces the money and tears it up*) I want a poem. I hope your shoes are full of blood. I want ... (*A silence. He looks at the moon*) The moon will be ... No! No! I don't want this thought! I want other people's thoughts. I want thoughts that have been thought already. But I can see it. The moon. We looked up and asked. Wonder and mystery. Home of the gods. The goddess moon. Magic. Healer. Cheap songs for sweethearts. The moon in June. By the silvery light of. We turned our faces to it, bathed our faces in it, watched it through the door. But soon they'll bring pieces of her back. We'll know what type of rock, what dust, she is. Even then we'll still sing her. The footprint and the flag won't disturb the poetry. We'll still look up as the ancients did. The same moon. But soon — no, no, don't let me think it — when the moon lifts low on the horizon and she is red, that will not be the goddess angry. That will be the people'd moon. The moon bearing her burden of the new colonies. The moon that is home to the further millions. And the blood will be flowing on her surface, just as it flows here. How can we delight in her light when we know that blood flows there?

Soldier Two enters

Soldier Two So you're back.
Soldier One I never went away.
Soldier Two Were you crying?
Soldier One Why would you care?
Soldier Two We should move on.
Soldier One You'll only leave me.
Soldier Two I'll always be with you.
Soldier One Everyone goes.

The Daughter enters. She looks about her

Soldier Two I recognize that one.
Soldier One No you don't, you weren't there. I was there. I got the goats, sold the gun. You made up filthy lies, put them in my head. (*Calling*) Hey! You! Tell him I didn't hide. Tell him there was no raping and killing.

Daughter I tried to find the city.
Soldier One Tell him.
Daughter The city wasn't there. There was a hole in the ground. Going on for ever. A crater.
Soldier One Sorry to hear it. About that night when ——
Daughter Who are you?
Soldier Two The peach tree. Your father in the branches — he told me ...
Soldier One You keep out of this. (*To the Daughter*) He tried to make me remember something that I never did. I've my good name to think of. Think. Did I hide in a cupboard when the bastards came?
Daughter I managed to save these. (*She produces a twisted knife and a fork*) Whole buildings had melted.
Soldier One If it's grub you're after, we've not a crumb.
Soldier Two A peach tree and I was ...
Soldier One I *told* you about the peach tree. You were not there. It's my memory, my words. Now, miss, if we could clear up the matter of ——
Daughter It was cherry blossom time. The cherry blossom should have been out in the city. The trees looked like skeletons. Or was it the other way round? Did the skeletons look like ...
Soldier One She's barking.
Soldier Two Trees like skeletons. There were trees like that, in the war. Sticking out of the mud. Stumps.
Soldier One The war? Oh, yes ...
Soldier Two No birds singing.
Daughter No birds singing in the city. Dead fish in the river.

The Prison Guard enters. He has a notepad, pen, a chart and measuring instruments. He is measuring out the ground

Soldier One Hallo there. How did the poem go down?
Guard (*counting*) Ten ... twenty ... thirty kilometres. (*He jots the figure down*) She divorced me.
Soldier One Shame.
Guard (*consulting his chart*) Ninety degrees west ... Fifty kilometres. (*He measures a new angle during the following*)
Soldier One Big structure going up? A — palace? A — hospital? Give us a clue.
Guard More than my job's worth,
Soldier One Why did she divorce you?
Guard She tore the poem up. She wanted something with moon in it.
Soldier One That must've been a blow.
Guard I had a nervous breakdown. Lost my job.
Soldier One There's a moral there ...

Guard Ended up here.
Soldier One Yes. "Stay clear of poetry if you want to keep your wife."

The Daughter attacks the measuring instruments with the knife, trying to damage them

Guard Little bitch!
Daughter Don't you know what it's for? Did they tell you?
Guard It's the only work I could get.
Daughter And they're building a railway. Coming right here. Stops here. Gates.
Soldier Two We could take a ride.
Daughter Your last one. (*She attacks again, trying to damage the instruments*)
Guard Now you're for it …
Soldier Two Why my last? How do you know?
Soldier One (*looking out*) Yes. There's a train. Full of people.

They all look out

    No. Just sand blowing about. For a moment …
Soldier Two So much sand.

They all look

Soldier One So much space.
Soldier Two So hot.
Soldier One Like a furnace.
Soldier Two And the moon.

They look up

Soldier One Red.
Soldier Two Harvest moon.
Soldier One Harvest moon?
Soldier Two When they burn the stubble. When the moon is low. The smoke from the stubble rises up. The moon turns red.
Soldier One There is no stubble. There's been no harvest here. What would grow here?
Daughter There will be a harvest. Such a harvest!
Soldier One Like the city became a crater? She's got bats in the belfry.

    The Prisoner enters

Prisoner I have no food. But I have a story. I will tell my story if you will give me some food.

The others find the Prisoner's story increasingly amusing as it progresses; by the end they are all laughing hysterically

Two oranges. A carton of milk. A loaf of bread. An onion. A bar of chocolate. Two oranges. Soldiers in the distance. A carton of milk. A line of soldiers in the distance. A loaf of bread. A line of soldiers in the distance closing ranks. An onion. A line of soldiers in the distance closing ranks and raising their guns. A bar of chocolate. A line of soldiers in the distance closing their ranks and raising their guns in the square. A tank rolls into the square. Two oranges. I am in the square. A carton of milk. I am in the square. A loaf of bread. I am in the square. An onion. I am in the square. A bar of chocolate. I am in the square.

Daughter (*pointing*) The train. The train.

They look out

Soldier Two No ... No ...
Daughter But soon — soon.
Soldier One (*to Soldier Two*) Come on. Last leg.
Soldier Two North?
Soldier One Home and dry we'll be.
Soldier Two You and me?
Soldier One Peas in a pod.
Soldier Two But what if ——
Soldier One No buts and ifs. Off we go.

The Soldiers exit

Daughter (*calling*) Remember. The arrival is the start of another journey.
Soldier Two (*off; calling*) That's a very bad translation.

The Lights fade

SCENE 7

A border post

Soldier One and Soldier Two are on their own

Soldier One It's a bloody cheek. Keeping us waiting.

Soldier Two Paperwork.
Soldier One We won the sodding war for them.
Soldier Two It's the same the world over.
Soldier One Trekked all the way here and then they ——
Soldier Two Won't be long now.
Soldier One They didn't even offer a cup of tea.

A Military Cop (Cop One) enters, looking at documents

Cop One Why did it take you so long?
Soldier One South to north, it's a long way.
Cop One Stuck together? All the way?
Soldier One Like barnacles to a rock. Hey, that's a new one.
Soldier Two I'll jot it down. (*He produces his notebook and writes in it*)
Soldier One (*to the Cop*) I never used to speak in metaphor. Never heard of
the word. Meta-phor. Lovely word. Now they come out all over the place.
Cop One (*taking Soldier Two's notebook*) What's this?
Soldier Two A diary. My thoughts.
Cop One (*reading*) "Imperious Caesar, dead and turned to clay,
Might stop a hole to keep the wind away."
Soldier One "O, that that earth, which kept the world in awe,
Should patch a wall t'expel the winter's flaw!"
Cop One Did he teach you that?
Soldier One It just comes naturally these days. I was useless at school.
They'll not believe their ears when I get home.
Cop One The word's "if".
Soldier One If?

The Cop takes Soldier One to one side

Cop One Converse a lot, did you, on the way?
Soldier One Oh, we nattered, yes we did.
Cop One About?
Soldier One This and that.
Cop One Don't generalize.
Soldier One I know. To generalize is to be a fool. Someone said that. I always
used to generalize. Which is a generalization in itself. Can't you just stamp
our papers and get us back to our units?
Cop One Don't you realize?
Soldier One What?
Cop One Don't you know?
Soldier One More than I did. I came up with the Theory of Relativity the
other day. But I knew someone must've got there before me.

Cop One The danger you're in.
Soldier One I'm out of it now. I'm home. I'm north.
Cop One With *him*.
Soldier One My pal. We fought the common enemy then we walked up from
the south together.
Cop One My point. Talking. You talked. You told him things. He wrote
things down. You'd better keep your trap shut.

Cop Two enters

This'un's all right, sir.
Cop Two (*looking at Soldier Two*) That one?
Cop One (*showing the documents to Cop Two*) He'll be for the loading up.
Cop Two (*whispering*) Nasty business. Nasty scenes down at the railhead.
Cop One Still, he'll be with his own kind. He'll want to go home.
Cop Two The last batch were screaming blue murder.
Soldier Two Excuse me, but ——
Cop One No buts. You both wait here. (*To Soldier One*) And remember the
ifs.

The Cops exit

Soldier One Rum do.
Soldier Two He took my book.
Soldier One We've been away a long time. How long, d'you reckon?
Soldier Two What did he say to you?
Soldier One That I was in ... Not much.
Soldier Two They said I had to be loaded.
Soldier One What'll you do — now it's all in the bag?
Soldier Two Perhaps I should have stayed, perhaps I should not have run
away.
Soldier One When?
Soldier Two After the Great Change. But when the war came, I did join the
battalion. Now that I have fought for my country, perhaps they would be
... Loaded. On to what, I wonder? What are they doing?
Soldier One They've got to be careful. That's it. In case we're not really us.
In case we're really from the other side. You know. Disguised, trying to
sneak past. Once they've gone through it all they'll realize. We'll be fine.
Soldier Two How do you know?
Soldier One Because it wouldn't make sense otherwise.

The Lights fade

SCENE 8

A prison visiting-room

The Girl is visiting the Woman

Girl How are they treating you?
Woman Why should you care?
Girl I wanted to ——
Woman They mended your ear.
Girl They can work miracles these days. I'm sorry about your babies. I'm never going home. I mean, I went home. I told my father I had been to the place where my great-grandfather had been a boy.
Woman Did he pay for the ear? You're very pretty.
Girl When they let you out …
Woman I will make my way to the coast. There I will find work cleaning the rooms of the tourists. No-one will know me.
Girl We could go somewhere. Together.
Woman Free like the birds?
Girl I tried to explain to my father about the babies. He likes poetry, just like my great- grandfather. I read something to him. (*She takes out the notebook and reads*)
                    "Be as thou wast wont to be;
                    See as thou wast wont to see.
                    Dian's bud o'er Cupid's flower
                    Hath such force and blessed power."
Woman And it did not work?
Girl That's when I knew.
Woman You thought poetry would clean his eyes. Foolish child. Poetry has no power. Your father does not want to imagine my babies. That would spoil his dreams. And his new suits. I can say poems in your language. I still cut away your ear. Where would I go with you?
Girl I can never remember poems. Just pop songs.

The Lights fade

SCENE 9

A railway station

Soldier Two is on his own, with his knapsack

Soldier One and Cop One enter. The Cop is carrying Soldier Two's notebook and a spare gun. They stand at a distance. The Cop hands the gun to Soldier One

Cop Do what they said. They've got their eye on you.
Soldier One He's my pal.
Cop They need to be sure of you.
Soldier One Some other way. There must be.
Cop No other way.
Soldier One If he is sent back they will ——
Cop We are not politicians.
Soldier One He fought for them. All the exiles, they fought for their country.
He has proved his loyalty.
Cop The politicians have made their settlements.
Soldier One The war's over.
Cop You're still under orders. You must be seen to be loyal.
Soldier One Loyal?
Cop Just do it. (*He hands the book to Soldier Two*) Quite a scribbler, eh?

The Cop exits

There is the sound of goatbells

The Goatboy enters

Soldier Two Greetings my friend. Not losing your goats any more?
Goatboy I'm chief herder for the district now.
Soldier Two My congratulations.
Goatboy (*waving at the goats*) On you go! On you go!

Soldier One moves to Soldier Two

Soldier Two You remember our friend with the goats?
Soldier One The one who could have been our son?
Goatboy They don't want to get into the wagons. (*He waves*) Go on! I'll put
a boot up their backsides. (*He watches the goats*)
Soldier Two (*looking at the gun*) So it's been decided. Well. You have a
family to think of. These things are out of our hands. And they need to be
sure of you. We were walking together for a long time. So I mustn't go
quietly, must I? Or they will suspect there is something between us. We
must show them there is nothing between us. We must show them there is
hatred between us.
Soldier One But where will they send you? Will you end up in a lime-pit?
Soldier Two If I'm out of luck. If not, there are places they send folk.
Soldier One What sort of places?
Soldier Two Where the earth is always frozen. Where it's always night.
There will be the moon to look at. Poems to be made. Now then, you must
do it. Don't let them imagine the worst.

Soldier One What is the worst they could — imagine?
Soldier Two That we are friends. That would not do. I will scream and pretend to struggle. You will force me into the wagon with all the others. There may even be some blood. Just enough to convince them. I will plead with you. You may beat me over the head if you need to.
Soldier One Thank you.
Soldier Two My pleasure. Now we will struggle a little. That will be our embrace. And I will pass you my book. Come now.

Soldier One embraces Soldier Two. They shift a little

More effort. Now the book. (*He slips the book into Soldier One's pocket*) Order me on to the train.
Soldier One On to the train.
Soldier Two Say it louder and say "you bastard".
Soldier One You bastard!
Soldier Two "With the other scum".
Soldier One With the other scum!

The Girl and the Woman enter from the opposite direction to that taken by the Cop; they head across the station

During the following, the two pairs cross through each other but do not see each other

Girl Did the journey tire you?
Woman I like to ride in trains.
Girl Shall we stay in this city for a while?
Woman I should like to see it.
Soldier Two Keep shoving me.
Soldier One They'll never get you all in that wagon.
Soldier Two I had a dream last night.
Soldier One I know. It was an old man.
Soldier Two You. Going through a door. Push me harder. Insult me.
Soldier One (*pushing harder*) Pig!
Soldier Two Louder.
Soldier One Vermin!
Woman Such a grand station.
Girl Restored to its original grandeur, says the guidebook.
Woman Such architecture.
Soldier Two And coming through the door, the other way, towards you ...
Soldier One A baby.
Soldier Two You passed each other.

Soldier One Briefly.
Woman So many people.
Girl Not so many.
Woman Yes, yes, can't you see them all? Where are they all going?

There is the sound of goatbells

Goatboy Shoo! Shoo!
Girl Let's get going. The museum closes in an hour.
Soldier One Why am I doing this?
Soldier Two Give me your right hand. So it looks like we are fighting.

Soldier One gives Soldier Two his right hand

There.
Soldier One Does it say why?
Soldier Two No. It says what you are doing.
Woman Why are you doing this?

There is the sound of goatbells

THE END

FURNITURE AND PROPERTY LIST

ACT I

SCENE 1

On stage: "Fire"
Battered tin can of food
Spoon
Canvas knapsack. *In it*: tin water bottle, piece of sausage
Heavy rifle

Off stage: Rifle, and knapsack containing piece of hard cheese, piece of dry bread
(**Soldier Two**)

Personal: **Soldier One**: packet of cigarettes, ragged cloth map
Soldier Two: small notebook and pencil, compass

SCENE 2

On stage: Backpack for **Girl**

Personal: **Girl**: street map, worn notebook
Man: cigarette

SCENE 3

On stage: Three pebbles; one red, one white, one black

SCENE 4

Personal: **Girl**: blindfold

SCENE 5

No additional props

SCENE 6

On stage: Chair
Plate of food for **Daughter**

Personal: **Daughter**: folded piece of cloth containing banknotes
               Father: document

SCENE 7

No additional props

SCENE 8

No additional props

SCENE 9

On stage: Melon pip

SCENE 10

On stage: **Girl**'s wallet containing newspaper cutting for **Man**

Personal: **Man**: knife

SCENE 11

Off stage: Coolbag containing bottle of mineral water (**Archaeologist One**)
               Backpacks containing sieve, magnifying glass, little brush
               (**Archaeologists**)

Personal: **Archaeologist One**: document, chart
               Militia person: pistol

ACT II

SCENE 1

Personal: **Girl**: bandage

SCENE 2

On stage: Rusty nail
               Chains for **Prisoner**

SCENE 3

On stage: Table with microphone
               Chair

SCENE 4

Personal: **Soldier One**: money

SCENE 5

Off stage: Torch (**Tour Guide**)

SCENE 6

Off stage: Twisted knife, fork (**Daughter**)
                Measuring instruments, notebook/pad/piece of paper, pencil/pen, chart
                (**Prison Guard**)

SCENE 7

Off stage: Documents (**Military Cop**)

SCENE 8

No additional props

SCENE 9

Off stage: Spare gun (**Cop**)

LIGHTING PLOT

Practical fittings required: wood fire
Various simple interior and exterior settings

ACT I, SCENE 1

To open: General exterior lighting; bright, with no shade. Wood fire effect on

Cue 1	**Soldier Two** yawns and sleeps *Fade lights to black-out; cut fire effect*	(Page 5)

ACT I, SCENE 2

To open: General exterior lighting

Cue 2	The **Woman** and the **Man** carry the **Girl** off *Fade lights to black-out*	(Page 7)

ACT I, SCENE 3

To open: General exterior lighting; cold dawn effect

Cue 3	The **Goatboy** exits *Fade lights to black-out*	(Page 11)

ACT I, SCENE 4

To open: General interior lighting

Cue 4	**Girl**: "I'm not an animal." *Fade lights to black-out*	(Page 11)

ACT I, SCENE 5

To open: General exterior lighting

Cue 5	**Soldier Two** falls asleep *Fade lights to black-out*	(Page 13)

ACT I, SCENE 6

To open: General interior lighting

| *Cue* 6 | The **Daughter** exits. The **Goatboy** is left
Fade lights to black-out | (Page 18) |

ACT I, SCENE 7

To open: General exterior lighting

| *Cue* 7 | **Soldier Two** curls up and sleeps
Fade lights to black-out | (Page 18) |

ACT I, SCENE 8

To open: General interior lighting

| *Cue* 8 | The **Man** blindfolds the **Girl**
Fade lights to black-out | (Page 20) |

ACT I, SCENE 9

To open: General exterior lighting

| *Cue* 9 | The **Soldiers** dig
Fade lights to black-out | (Page 23) |

ACT I, SCENE 10

To open: General exterior lighting

| *Cue* 10 | **Man**: " ... merely history unwinding."
Fade lights to black-out | (Page 24) |

ACT I, SCENE 11

To open: General exterior lighting

| *Cue* 11 | **Archaeologist One**: " ... Gave Battle In Vain."
Fade lights to black-out | (Page 31) |

Lighting Plot

ACT II, SCENE 1

To open: General interior lighting

Cue 12	**Girl**: "… died with it." *Fade lights to black-out*	(Page 31)

ACT II, SCENE 2

To open: General interior lighting but not on Prisoner

Cue 13	**Soldier One**: "What's this?" *Bring up lights on* **Prisoner**	(Page 34)
Cue 14	**Soldier One**: " … *an original thought?*" *Fade lights to black-out*	(Page 39)

ACT II, SCENE 3

To open: General interior lighting

Cue 14	**Girl**: " … they are our own?" *Fade lights to black-out*	(Page 39)

ACT II, SCENE 4

To open: General exterior lighting with moonlight

Cue 15	The **Soldiers** sleep *Fade lights to black-out*	(Page 42)

ACT II, SCENE 5

To open: General interior lighting to suggest a dark cave

Cue 16	**Guide**: "Still fresh." *Fade lights to black-out*	(Page 43)

ACT II, SCENE 6

To open: General exterior lighting with moonlight

Cue 17	**Soldier Two**: "That's a very bad translation." *Fade lights to black-out*	(Page 47)

ACT II, Scene 7

To open: General exterior lighting

Cue 18   **Soldier One**: " ... wouldn't make sense otherwise."   (Page 49)
              Fade lights to black-out

ACT II, SCENE 8

To open: General interior lighting

Cue 19   **Girl**: "Just pop songs."   (Page 50)
              Fade lights to black-out

ACT II, SCENE 9

To open: General interior lighting

No cues

EFFECTS PLOT

ACT I

Cue 1	The **Soldiers** make to go *Distant goatbells*	(Page 9)
Cue 2	**Soldier One**: "If they bag you, I'm stuck." Pause *Gunshot*	(Page 10)
Cue 3	**Soldier One** crawls off; pause *Gunshot*	(Page 11)
Cue 4	**Soldier Two**: " …but a long moment." *Goatbells*	(Page 12)
Cue 5	**Daughter**: "Something that will benefit us all." *Goatbells*	(Page 15)

ACT II

Cue 6	**Soldier Two**: "… or a torture chamber." *Sounds of bolts and locks*	(Page 32)
Cue 7	The **Cop** exits *Goatbells*	(Page 51)
Cue 8	**Woman**: "Where are they all going?" *Goatbells*	(Page 53)
Cue 9	**Woman**: "Why are you doing this?" *Goatbells*	(Page 53)